Hans Andersen's Denmark

Hans Andersen's Denmark *described in*

PICTURES AND TEXT

Text by Mogens Knudsen

Pictures selected by Chr. Bang

Illustrationsforlaget COPENHAGEN 1950

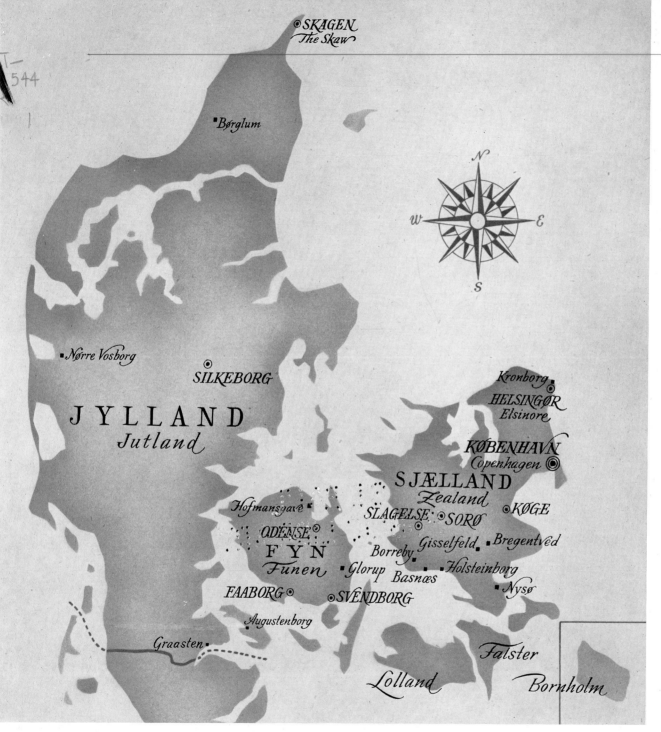

Map of Denmark
showing all the
towns, castles,
and manor-houses
mentioned in
the book.

PORTRAIT MASK OF HANS ANDERSEN ABOVE A WINDOW
AT CHRISTIANSBORG CASTLE. BY A. BUNDGAARD

Contents

(25) *Elsinore. Old House in Strandgade.*
52, Strandgade, half-timbered house, 1781.

(26) *Kronborg Castle seen from the Harbour of Elsinore.*

(27) *Kronborg Castle. Moat.*

(28) *Kronborg Castle. From the Casemates.*

(29) *Copenhagen. Amalienborg Castle.*
The palace square with the four similar pala·ces which form the castle (built 1749·60) is considered the main Danish architectural work in Rococo style. Like the equestrian statue of Frederick V. (erected in 1768, the work of the French sculptor Jacques Saly) it enjoys European fame. Since Christiansborg Castle was burnt down in 1794 Amalienborg has been the residence of the Danish royal family. — The colonnade connecting two of the palaces (the columns to be seen in the foreground of the picture) was added in 1795.

(30) *Copenhagen. Hans Andersen's Room in Vingaardsstræde.*
No. 6, Vingaardsstræde.

(31) *Funen. Hulgade in Svendborg.*
The Seaport of Svendborg in South Funen. (22,000 inhabitants).

(32-33) *Funen. The Voigtske Gaard in Faaborg, and Funen. View of Faaborg from the Harbour.*
Faaborg in South Funen (5,000 inhabitants). — Rich in half-timbered buildings from the 18th century. — "Agent Voigts Gaard", No. 1, Vestergade, from about 1730.

(34) *Funen. The Manor-House of Hofmansgave.*
In North-East Funen, on Odense Fjord. — The main building in late Rococo style; the wings are half-timbered; from about 1784.

(35) *Funen. The Manor-House of Glorup.*
In South-East Funen. — Baroque style, 1743·44. — Portal and ridge turret from 1762-65.

(36) *Farm in Zealand.*
This small farm with a main building and two wings is typical of Zealand.

(37) *Zealand. The Manor-House of Gisselfeld.*
In South-East Zealand. — Renaissance style, 1547-75.

(38) *Zealand. Park of the Manor-House of Bregentved.*
In South-East Zealand. — The present appearance of the main building is due to its being almost completely rebuilt after Hans Andersen's death (1886-91).

(39) *Zealand. Gate at the Manor-House of Basnæs.*
In South-West Zealand. The main building is from 1846. — The barn gate shown here is from 1850. The relief, dated 1638, has been transferred from one of the buildings of the earlier Basnæs.

(40) *Zealand. The Manor-House of Borreby.*
In South-West Zealand. — Early Renaissance style with partly medieval characteristics, built in 1586. Fortified castle with a watchman's gallery and holes for pouring boiling water or tar on attackers.

(41) *Zealand. The Manor-House of Holsteinborg.*
On the South-West coast of Zealand. — 1598 and 1639-49. — The picture shows the west wing completed in 1649. The original gables in Renaissance style were changed into Gothic style in 1848. — In the park there is an ivy which Hans Andersen is said to have planted.

(42) *Zealand. Scenery near Holsteinborg.*

(43) *The Island of Glænö off Holsteinborg.*

(44-45) *Zealand. From the Garden of Nysö and The Manor-House of Nysö.*
In South-East Zealand. — The main building, in Dutch Baroque style, was built in 1673 — The pavilion in the garden was erected on the site of a studio built for Bertel Thorvald·sen (1768-1844). Contains works of the sculptor. In the main building there is also a collection of works of Thorvaldsen.

(46) *South Jutland. Augustenborg Castle.*
Situated on the island of Als belonging to Slesvig. — The main building 1770-76. The picture shows the central part of the main building with a fronton in which the monogram of the builder, Duke Frederick Christian, is engraved on an escutcheon surrounded by war attributes. The castle is now a hospital.

(47) *South Jutland. Graasten Castle.*
Built in Baroque style at the beginning of the 18th century, but the greater part destroyed by fire in 1757. Later rebuilt and altered at various times.

(48) *Jutland. The Manor-House of Nörre Vosborg.*
The oldest part from the 16th century. The picture shows the south wing from 1838.

(49) *A Scene from Jutland.*
In the foreground a grave mound from Denmark's Bronze Age (ab. 1500-400 B. C.), in the background a medieval village church.

(50) *Jutland. The River Gudenaa near Silkeborg.*

(51) *From the West Coast of Jutland.*
Denmark has a coastline of 4,625 miles in all. For comparison it may be mentioned that the coastline of England and Wales amounts to 2,350 miles. The poets rightly sing of "sea-encircled Denmark".

(52) *Jutland. The Manor-House of Börglumkloster.*
From the early Middle Ages. Originally an episcopal residence and a Premonstratensian monastery, it was in the 17th century turned into a manor-house. The present buildings date back to the end of the 15th century, but in the 1750es were rebuilt according to the regular plan of the Baroque style, as they still appear today.

(53) *Jutland. From the Dunes of the Skaw.*

(54) *Copenhagen. The Round Tower.*
Built by King Christian IV. in 1637-43.

(55) *The Spiral Ramp in the Round Tower.*

(56) *Copenhagen. Street-sign in Hyskenstræde.*

(57) *Copenhagen. Old Roofs.*
From the quarter round Nicolai Church, where Andersen lived in various places. The towers in the background are, from the left: The Cathedral of Our Lady (cf. pictures 16 and 67), Saint Petri Church, and the Church of the Holy Ghost.

(58) *Copenhagen. The Former Frederick's Hospital.*
Built in Rococo style 1752-57. — Now containing the Danish Museum of Applied Art.

(59) *Copenhagen. From Frederiksberg Park.*

(60) *Copenhagen. House in Nyboder.*

(61) *Zealand. Old House in Köge.*
"Smedegaarden", 13, Store Kirkestræde Half-timbered house from the 16th century (the door from 1696, the two porch stones from ab. 1520).

(62) *Copenhagen. Vartov.*
27, Farvergade, close to Raadhuspladsen (the Town Hall Square). — Baroque style, 1724-54.

(63) *Copenhagen. Thorvaldsen's Tomb.*
Bertel Thorvaldsen the sculptor, 1768-1844 (cf. the text to pictures 44-45). The museum, which contains his work and in the courtyard of which he lies buried, was erected 1839-48 by the Danish architect M. G. B. Bindesböll in a highly personal neo-classical style. It is considered one of the most original architectural works of modern times. — In the foreground of the picture the "Angel of Baptism" by Thorvaldsen is seen.

(64) *Copenhagen. Sökvæsthuset in Christianshavn.*
58-64, Overgaden oven Vandet. — Rococo style, 1754-55.

(65) *Copenhagen. Nyhavn.*

(66) *Hans Andersen's Window, 20, Nyhavn.*

(67) *Copenhagen. The Cathedral of Our Lady.*
Founded towards the end of the 12th century. The church was set on fire during the bombardment of Copenhagen by the English in 1807. The present building was erected 1811-29 in neo-classical style.

(68) *Copenhagen. Hans Andersen's Tomb in Assistens Churchyard.*

PORTRAITS OF HANS ANDERSEN

ILLUSTRATIONS TO THE FAIRY-TALES FROM DIFFERENT COUNTRIES

FROM HANS ANDERSEN'S HOUSE ETC.

THUMBELINA. BY VILHELM PEDERSEN

FOREWORD

*Harmony, peace and simplicity —
these words are characteristic of most of
Hans Christian Andersen's wonderful
fairy tales and stories — and they are
characteristic too of the land of his birth, Denmark. Indeed the rare
genius of Andersen and the charm and beauty of Denmark are a
fitting combination. What a perfect setting for these immortal
tales — "The Ugly Duckling," "The Tinder Box," "The Steadfast
Tin Soldier," "Clumsy Hans," and "Little Claus and Big Claus."*

BEVERLY HILLS · CALIFORNIA · APRIL 1950

Jean Hersholt·

The reality behind
the fairy-tales

The kingdom of Denmark, in which the melancholy Prince Hamlet found in his day that there was "something rotten", lies hidden under the Scandinavian peninsula as beneath a sheltering roof. To the west the peninsula of Jutland shoots up like a tongue from the Central European mainland, and in the shelter of this natural bulwark against the stern North Sea lie all the five hundred greater and smaller islands which form the rest of the country. To the east, divided from southern Sweden only by a narrow sound, we have the largest island, Zealand, with the capital Copenhagen and with Hamlet's town of Elsinore, and between Zealand and Jutland lies the round and fertile island of Funen, with the old cathedral town of Odense. Here — in the country's geographical centre so to speak — was born in 1805 the Dane whose name is most widely known throughout the world, the fairy-tale writer Hans Christian Andersen, and his birthplace has become for Den-

mark what Stratford-on-Avon is for England. Here is to be found his big museum, which every year is visited by thousands of tourists from all over the world.

Hans Andersen did not need to travel far to find adventure. It lay in his own life. When, as an elderly man, he wrote his life story he began it with these words: "My life is a lovely story, so happy and full. Had I as a boy, when poor and alone I went out into the world, met a good fairy who had said: "Choose your own course and your goal in life and then, according to the development of your mind, it lies in the nature of things that I shall protect and guide you," my fate could not even then have been more happy. The story of my life will say to the world what it says to me: there is a loving God who directs all things for the best."

The devout childhood faith which was instilled into Hans Christian as a boy and which gave him an unshakeable confidence in his own lucky star, followed him until his death and was strengthened by the amazing course of his own life. He confirmed one of the nineteenth century's favourite ideas, the myth of the instinctive and conquering genius who springs up from the depths of the people like a glorious flower. At a time when the middle classes were still fighting against the last remnants of the feudal system, before the break-through of industrialism and democracy, it was a hard struggle for a poor boy to defy society's strict class divisions and break the monopoly of education which was held by the ruling classes.

The poor shoemaker's son Hans Christian from Odense

carried this struggle through to victory. He possessed the necessary hardiness and he had the faith in himself which is a necessary condition. When, as a fourteen year old boy, he packed his bundle to set out for the capital and challenge Fortune he had already in his naïve, precocious way marked out his future path and described it in these words: "One goes through dreadfully hard times first, and then one becomes famous."

He tasted both — both the hardship and the fame. But his path to the goal followed no straight line. It was both winding and stony. Many years passed before he realised in which way his special genius could best find expression. When his first collection "Fairy-Tales for Children" was published in 1835 neither he himself nor his contemporaries attached particular attention to these nursery stories. He himself strove towards "real" literature: plays, dramatic poems, novels, etc. Within these literary forms he won himself a fair reputation as a writer, but it is the fairy-tales which have entitled him to immortality.

It was also they which, in the course of a short time, carried his reputation beyond the country's frontiers, and not until he had acquired European fame were his own countrymen's eyes really opened to the national treasure they possessed in Hans Andersen's fairy-tales. They have conquered all over the world and they are still conquering. They are Denmark's greatest contribution to world literature, they have been translated into countless languages, they have forced their way far beyond the European sphere of culture, for instance to the oriental countries, so that the West has paid something in return for the rich treasury of fairy-tales which has been brought home from there throughout the ages.

Hans Andersen's fairy-tales are the first in the world which have been written for children, and they have still their most faithful readers among the millions of young people whose dreams they have fulfilled. But the fairy-tales belong to those rare works of art which with their charm captivate both young and old, both lay and learned. It is writing which has universal and eternal validity.

In Hans Andersen's life-time the fame of the fairy-tales went before him, and on his many journeys in Europe he was fêted wherever he went. He was the highly esteemed guest of kings and princes and he formed friendships with many famous Europeans. Among these was Charles Dickens, also a poor boy who had become one of literature's great men.

During his later years his popularity spread to the new world, several collections of his fairy-tales were published in U.S.A. and a few of the tales were printed in American magazines even before they were published in Danish. With his American translator, Horace E. Scudder, he carried on a cordial correspondence (this has lately been published by Jean Hersholt) and Scudder invited him several times to pay a visit to the States. Hans Andersen was a tireless traveller, and he would greatly have liked to accept Scudder's invitation, but he was at that time already too old and weak to dare to set out upon the long and exacting voyage.

He was also fêted in his own country. While still a very young man he had gained admission to several of the culturally and socially leading Copenhagen middle-class families. Later he found firm patrons among the nobility, and he spent countless holidays, both short and long, on their country estates. Most of his fairy-tales were written during these summer visits.

By his restless life of travel, by his association with people from all classes of society, and by a childlike joy in his own fame, Andersen was compensated for the lack of a home and family.

In reality he led a rather dreary bachelor existence. His mind was galled and irritable, he was boundlessly grateful for any kindness shown to him, but real or imagined slights and pin-pricks could throw him into the deepest despair. He was an artist of the type whose life is split between outward triumphs and personal defeats.

In this book we shall outline the main points in his life. We have chosen to do this by the help of a series of pictures of parts of the country and places which are associated with Hans Andersen's life or his writings. All the photographs in the main part of the book are modern and their subjects are generally accessible. It is an attempt to capture some features of Hans Andersen's Denmark which are still in existence to-day. The aim of the book has therefore been two-fold, first to tell the story of Hans Andersen and secondly to give an impression of Danish scenery and of the older Danish architecture which still sets its stamp on the country. An exhaustive picture of Denmark to-day must naturally not be expected. Modern Denmark is also something more and something different than these picturesque cottages and narrow streets and old castles. It is to just as great an extent characterised by co-operative dairies, slaughter-houses and cement factories, by fishing cutters and Diesel motor-ships, by steel bridges, cars, cycles and sports grounds, by Folk High Schools and public libraries. But in the industrialised everyday of the twentieth century the idyll of Hans Andersen enters as an indispensable part. One receives an idea of this on the king's birthday when all school-children have a holiday and the Royal Guard march in their red gala uniforms through the capital, and gold apples dance in the spray from the fountain in Gammeltorv.

It is features from this historical and yet living Denmark we have endeavoured to concentrate on in this series of pictures. Hans Andersen's fairy-tales have long ago become the whole world's possession, but it is natural that they are embraced with a special love by his own countrymen, whose temperament has been formed under the influence of those stories every child has read, and by that treasury of humour, irony, knowledge of human nature, sympathy, melancholy, and poetic feeling which is to be found there, and his verbal and animated style has influenced modern Danish.

The pictures can say nothing of all this. But they can give some idea of the background in time and milieu of these writings, which in their own subtle way give life and soul to the whole universe, all creation, even lifeless things.

With his vast imagination Hans Andersen draws a magic circle round both heaven and earth and lo: everything bends to his will. But his imagination was nourished by his own experience. Often his tales are built on ancient legends and traditional stories, but more often than not he draws his subject from a fragment of reality which he, with his extraordinarily sharp senses, had made his own. He is one of literature's greatest realists and in his tales can be found countless glimpses and sketches of incidents taken from the everyday life of his time, from the Danish landscape or from Danish history. The fairy-tales have universal validity, but besides they have nearly all local colour and bear the mark of the soil from which they sprang. From his upbringing in various parts of the country, and later from his many travels, he was familiar with nearly all the districts of his native country, and in his books is to be found a more comprehensive and many-coloured picture of Denmark than has been given, either before or later, by any other writer.

"*Who knows, but I may be so successful that in the geography book will be written:*

Odense, here the writer Hans Andersen was born".

(Letter from Hans Andersen 1837)

HERLUF LYKKE

1. Hans Andersen's Statue behind St. Knud's Cathedral in Odense

In ancient Greece seven cities laid claim to being the birthplace of the poet Homer. In Odense the exact house where Hans Andersen was born has been disputed. The question is still undecided. An unauthenticated tradition has pointed out an old cottage in *Hans Jensensstræde* in the poor quarter of old Odense — he was actually born in this quarter — as the birthplace of the fairy-tale writer, and here the big museum has been built, which together with the old corner-house contains the largest collection of Hans Andersen relics to be found in the country.

2. Odense. "H. C. Andersens Hus" (Hans Andersen's house), Hans Jensensstræde

Odense is one of the oldest market-towns in Denmark. In 1805, when Hans Andersen was born, it was the second largest town in the country, but it had, nevertheless, no more than 3,000 inhabitants. Today the population is more than 100,000 and the town has, of course, changed in appearance, but many old buildings still bear witness of the past. The many large houses belonging

3. Odense. Old Cottages

HERLUF LYKKE

4. *Odense. Nobleman's House, Möntestræde*

to merchants and wealthy citizens testify to Odense's reputation as an enterprising commercial town. It was the well-to-do middle classes and the nobility of Funen which set the tone for the life of the town. Hans Andersen was the son of a poor shoemaker and grew up on the less sunny side of society, but he received a many-hued crowd of impressions during his youth, and in his later writings he has reproduced both the atmosphere of the province and described

5. Merchant's House in Odense

many of the figures he met in his childhood. He has made his native town famous in literature and Odense showed him her gratitude during his life-time. On his birthday in 1867 he received the freedom of the city. A celebration, in magnificent style, was held for him in the town-hall, and on that day a prophecy, made to him in his boyhood by an old woman, was fulfilled. She had told him that Odense should one day be illuminated in his honour.

HERLUF LYKKE

6. Odense. Hans Andersen's Childhood Home in Munkemöllestræde

Hans Andersen's exact birthplace is unknown, but we know for certain the house which formed the frame round his dearest early memories. The little family moved to the low, single-storied, half-timbered house in *Munkemöllestræde* near the cathedral, when Hans, the only child of the marriage, was two years old, and he lived here until he was fourteen, a short time before he left Odense.

HERLUF LYKKE

7. The Living Room in Hans Andersen's Childhood Home

This is the little living-room, which together with a kitchen formed their home. Hans's father had his shoemaker's shop here and the rest of the space was nearly all taken up by his parents' bed and the turn-up bedstead where he slept. Their circumstances were poor and humble, but the boy received only love and tenderness from his parents. His father read him fairy-tales and comedies and made him a dolls' theatre for which he himself later wrote plays. The greatest experiences of his childhood were when his parents took him on a rare visit to the theatre in Odense. For a long time these visits would occupy his imagination, and they influenced him in directing his longings towards success on the stage.

HERLUF LYKKE

8. The Backyard of Hans Andersen's Childhood Home

Hans grew into a tall, awkward boy who lived in the world of his own imagination. Behind the house was a yard with an extremely unpretentious garden. It consisted, in fact, of only a single gooseberry bush. Here Hans would spread out his mother's apron with the help of a broom-handle. It was his tent in sunshine and rain; he would sit and gaze into the gooseberry bush and let his thoughts and dreams wander far away.

Within the bounds of his own home the strange and imaginative boy felt himself safe, but among companions of his own age he never felt secure from jeers and teasing. He was like "The Ugly Duckling" who had to be pecked because he was so large and odd. He found his best playmates among little girls, but he preferred, above all, the old women who told him folk-stories and legends. His parents could not afford to give him a proper schooling. He was sent to the *Charity School,* where the teaching was poor. It was not until many years later that he learned to spell passably, and he never really mastered the art.

HERLUF LYKKE

9. Odense. The Charity School in Paaskestræde

HERLUF LYKKE

10. Odense. St. Knud's Cathedral

Hans Andersen's father was something of a dreamer himself. He enlisted in the army and was away from home for two years. When he returned he was ill and his spirit was broken, and he died when his son was eleven years old. Responsibility for the maintenance of the home now rested entirely on the mother. She did washing for the better class families in the town, and in all kinds of weather stood with her scrubbing-board at Odense river. In memory of her he wrote the story "She was good for nothing" — a story full not only of a son's love but also of social bitterness. Odense river appears in many of his other fairy-tales as well, for example in "Thumbelina" and even more clearly in "The Bell Deep", which is built on the legend of a deep pool in the river near *St. Knud's Cathedral*.

Hans Andersen had reached the age of fourteen and his mother had to have him put to some kind of work. He could not go on loafing around. In the meantime he was confirmed in *St. Knud's Cathedral*. For ambitious reasons he joined the group which otherwise was composed of children from the better families, but he was tormented, in return, by a feeling of having pushed himself in where he did not belong. On this solemn occasion he got for the first time a pair of new boots, and so great was his childlike joy that he drew the tops up over his trousers to impress the whole congregation. But he suffered cruel pangs of conscience from the fact that his thoughts wandered in these worldly paths and did not concentrate on God.

HERLUF LYKKE

11. Odense. St. Knud's Cathedral

He had succeeded in interesting some of the wealthier citizens in himself, and he carried it so far that he was summoned to *Odense Castle* to appear before Prince Christian Frederick, the later King Christian the Eighth, who at that time was governor of Funen. But what was to be done with this strange youth, of whose real talents no one could have any idea? The Prince advised him to learn a sound trade. But this did not appeal to him. He was determined to go his own way and to become famous and that was impossible in Odense. He would have to go out into the wide world.

12. Odense Castle

ELLEN OG CARL JOH. JØRGENSEN

13. Funen. Mill Pond

Naïve and inexperienced as he was he made his big decision. He had collected a few shillings together and, on the fourth of September 1819, when he was fourteen years old, he packed his little bundle, put on the suit in which he had been confirmed, and set out for the capital, where he did not know a single soul. As a cheap-fare passenger on the day-coach he rolled out of Odense and further on through the countryside of *Funen*, with which he was familiar from so many excursions in his childhood. Funen is one of the most fertile of all Danish islands. The countryside is hilly and varied, luxuriant fields alternate with woods and meadows,

AAGE KNUDSEN

and the eye is arrested especially b
the quickset hedges which run along
side the roads and form the bound
aries between the fields. A sight spe
cially characteristic of Funen is th
broad low-trunked willow-tree, whicl
made such an impression on Han
Andersen's imagination that it late
appears in many places in his fairy
tales. Later on he came to know

ELLEN OG CARL JOH. JØRGENSEN

15. Funen. The Country-side at Harvest Time

nearly all aspects of the Danish landscape, but he continued to feel most at home with the mild and gentle scenery which he had come to know as a child. He prefers to describe it in summer-time, when everything glows with warmth and life, as it does at the beginning of "The Ugly Duckling", one of his most famous stories: "It was so beautiful out in the country. It was summer — the wheat fields were golden, the oats were green, and down among the meadows the hay was stacked. There the stork minced about on his red legs, clacking away in Egyptian, which was the language his mother had taught him. Round about the field and meadow lands rose vast forests, in which deep lakes lay hidden —."

16. Copenhagen. View of the Town from the Round Tower

Early one morning, after a two days' journey, Hans Andersen reached *Copenhagen*. From a hill in one of the suburbs he gazed, overwhelmed, at the spires and towers of the capital, and burst into tears at the thought that he was alone and friendless. Copenhagen, the city he was to conquer, was not only the country's largest town and the king's residence; it was besides the centre of art and culture. The university and academy of art lay here as well as the higher colleges, and first and foremost The Royal Theatre, the national stage, around which all Hans Andersen's dreams of the future were concentrated.

Measured by modern standards Copenhagen was, at that time, a small town which did not cover a tenth of the area which it occupies to-day. The streets were cobbled, and at nightfall the oil lamps shone with their sleepy gleam. Large parts of the old ramparts and moats which encompassed the city like a strait-jacket, and which were demolished less than a hundred years ago, are still in existence. They have now been turned into parks. In the evening the town-gates were closed, and those who had not reached the town in time, had to wait outside until the next morning. In the streets the watchmen went around during the night watching over peace and order and every hour they sang the old verses from the 17th century which stated what hour had struck.

17. Copenhagen. The Moat of Kastellet (The Citadel).

AAGE KNUDSEN

18. Copenhagen. Staircase in No. 19, Bredgade

Hans Andersen tried at once to storm the theatre. Dressed in his altered confirmation suit and with a big hat which fell down over his eyes, he called on the ballet dancer, Madame Schall, who had an elegant home at No. 19 in the fashionable street *Bredgade*. Before he dared to ring the bell he fell on his knees on the steps and prayed to God for protection. A passing servant-girl thought he was a beggar and handed him a coin. When he was ushered in to the dancer he immediately began to sing and dance to show his accomplishments, but the thin, overgrown youth with the naïve behaviour and the strange gestures did not make a favourable impression. The lady thought he was mad, and hurried him out.

There now followed a time marked by need and poverty. He obtained lodgings in one of Copenhagen's notorious quarters, but his ignorance of the world prevented him from realising what was going on around him. He called on the manager of the Royal Theatre and was turned away, but he succeeded, nevertheless, in entering the theatre by a roundabout way. He worked tirelessly at making the acquaintance of influential people and he came into touch with the composer Weyse, who received him in his home in *No. 8, Kronprinsessegade.* Weyse, who himself had been a poor boy, started a subscription for him; he got a little free tuition in singing and diction, and gradually he got a foothold inside the walls of the theatre. He was admitted to the ballet school and got a chance to appear on the stage a few times, though only as a supernumerary.

AAGE KNUDSEN

19. Copenhagen. No. 8, Kronprinsessegade

AAGE KNUDSEN

The old theatre from Hans Andersen's time has long since been replaced by a larger building. To see a stage such as he trod, you must visit the former *Court Theatre,* which is now a theatre museum, at Christiansborg Castle. In the beginning of the nineteenth century the Royal Theatre had its rehearsal room and ballet school here, and the old worn staircase, the artistes' ascent to the stage, seemed to Hans Andersen's imagination the symbol of the road upwards to light and fame. But the road was arduous. After a short time he was dismissed from the theatre. In spite of his youth he was active as a poet. He submitted several tragedies to the theatre, but he promptly got them back again. To all appearances he had suffered defeat in Copenhagen.

20. Copenhagen. Staircase in the Court Theatre

But some of the members of the management of the theatre had been convinced that the indomitable half-grown youth possessed abilities which ought to be encouraged. They recommended him for a royal grant to enable him to attend a grammar school and make up for some of the book-learning which he so sadly lacked. In the autumn of 1822 Hans Andersen left Copenhagen again to begin as a pupil in the grammar school in the little market-town of Slagelse in West Zealand, a district rich in historical monuments. Among the objects which occupied his imagination, was *St. Anders's Cross,* the only wayside crucifix in existence from Catholic times, which was erected on a hill outside the town. He wandered here many times, and from the hill, in clear weather, he could see across the Great Belt to his native island of Funen.

HERLUF LYKKE

21. Saint Anders's Cross near Slagelse

OVE GRØNBECK

22. Ruins of the Monastery of Antvorskov near Slagelse

While Hans Andersen was in Slagelse the *Antvorskov ruins* were excavated, and he followed this work with lively interest. In the Middle Ages, Antvorskov was one of Denmark's largest monasteries; at the end of the 16th century it was turned into a royal castle, but it gradually lost its importance and fell into decay. — The years at Slagelse were otherwise a none too happy time for Hans Andersen. The seventeen year old youth had to start in the lowest class where he shared the school benches with ten year old boys, and the headmaster of the school, an eminent classical philologist, lacked understanding of his new pupil's sensitive and easily wounded nature. His jeers and teasing often drove Andersen to the verge of desperation.

Among the happier moments in these years were the free days in summer when he would walk over to the nearby market-town of *Sorö,* a little college town in an idyllic setting among woods and lakes. Here he formed friendships with some of the pupils who, like himself, were would-be poets, and he was received warmly and with understanding by the novelist and poet B. S. Ingemann, who was a few years older than he was and a teacher at the Academy. He gave Andersen back some of the self-confidence he was gradually losing during the daily drudgery at his lessons.

23. Sorö Lake with the Academy

Hans Andersen worked laboriously through his studies. A change occurred after three years when his headmaster was moved to another market-town in Zealand, *Elsinore,* and sugge- sted that his pupil accompany him. Although Andersen was not very eager to comply, he dared not, how- ever, set himself against the head- master's wishes, but in Elsinore the

24. *Elsinore. Old Houses*

relations between them became even worse than they had been in Slagelse. But Andersen gained something from the move to Elsinore. He never forgot to use his eyes wherever he went, and there was life and activity in the old seafaring town which for centuries had played an important role in Danish state economy because it was here that the king levied a toll on

25. Elsinore. Old House in Strandgade

26. Kronborg Castle seen from the Harbour of Elsinore

every ship which passed through the Sound between Zealand and Sweden. To supervise the collection of this toll and at the same time to keep the mastery of the Sound and the Baltic, King Frederick the Second had built on a headland near Elsinore, between the years 1574-84, the huge *Castle of Kronborg* in Dutch Renaissance style. Kronborg was for its time one of the strongest fortresses, and it enjoyed a reputation far and wide over Europe on account of its magnificent situation and rich ornamentation. Kronborg has, however,

become most famous as the scene of Shakespeare's drama "Hamlet". It was on Kronborg's battlements that the young Prince Hamlet met his father's ghost and was charged to revenge his death. In our own times a performance of the play is given every summer in the castle courtyard where famous actors, among them John Gielgud, Laurence Olivier and Michael Redgrave, have given their interpretations of the Hamlet character. Under Kronborg's ramparts stretches a net of deep and roomy casemates in several storeys. Down here, according to an

27. *Kronborg Castle. Moat*

ancient legend, the national hero Holger Danske sits sleeping. He is clad in iron and his long beard has grown fast to the marble table on which he rests his head. In his dreams he follows events in Denmark, but if the country falls into serious danger the old hero will awake to action and the sound of his sword will re-echo all over the world. Hans Andersen later based one of his stories on this legend.

28. Kronborg Castle. From the Casema

CHR. LARSEN

29. Copenhagen. Amalienborg Castle

During his dreary years at school in the provinces Hans Andersen kept in regular touch with his patrons in Copenhagen. Although he had pledged himself to concentrate on his school duties, he could not, however, always resist the temptation to give vent to his feelings in verse. When he visited Copenhagen during his holidays he read aloud and recited, and he received more praise than he used to get at school. During some of his visits to Copenhagen the poor schoolboy had a very distinguished residence - namely one of the palaces of *The Royal Castle of Amalienborg* which at that time was a cadet school.

AAGE KNUDSEN

30. Hans Andersen's Room in Vingaardsstrœde

At long last Hans Andersen was permitted to leave school and his headmaster, who was, however, scarcely such a tormentor as Andersen has later described him. He moved to Copenhagen and took private tuition, and in 1828 he finally attained his goal — the laboriously achieved matriculation. In Copenhagen he had obtained lodgings in an attic in the centre of the town with a view over roofs and towers. The little room exists today almost unaltered. After passing his examination he now threw himself heart and soul into poetry and good fortune was with him. He had success with a few lesser literary works after the taste of the time and his name was suddenly on everyone's lips.

31. *Funen. Hulgade in Svendborg*

Later a period followed when criticism went hard aginst him and when he again nearly lost courage. But in the meantime the new-fledged poet was as happy as a lark. He drank freedom in long draughts and his head was full of plans. In the summer of 1830 he set out on a lengthy journey through Denmark in order to get to know his native land. The journey ended in southern Funen, a district which often appears in his stories and novels. — He passed through the seafaring town of *Svendborg,* with the steep, narrow streets, which he later compared to an Italian mountain town, and visited an old school-

friend whose father was a well-to-do merchant in another of the ports of southern Funen, *Faaborg.* — During this visit Andersen was struck by that fate which he has later described in the story of "The Naughty Boy" — Cupid with his arrow. He fell deeply in love with his friend's sister, Riborg Voigt, to whom he wrote the poem "I love thee dear", which to Grieg's music has become world famous. The young girl also grew fond of him, but she was betrothed to someone else,

32. Funen. The Voigtske Gaard in Faaborg

and their ways had to part. This first unhappy love-affair made a deep impression on Hans Andersen and brought out the melancholy side of his nature. He fell in love several times later. His love for the famous singer Jenny Lind, "the Swedish nightingale", inspired him to write the story "The Nightingale", but this love-affair too was hopeless. It must be supposed, however, that his love for Riborg Voigt was the one which left the deepest traces. After his death her farewell letter to him was found in a little leather purse hanging round his neck.

33. Funen. View of Faaborg from the Harbour

34. Funen. The Manor-House of Hofmansgave

About 1830 Hans Andersen began to be a regular guest at several of the manor-houses in Funen, first at Hofmansgave, later at Glorup. It was the opening of a special chapter of his life. As his reputation as a poet grew, and especially after the fairy-tales had made him famous, he became a much sought-after person socially, and he, who never had more than modest and often changing bachelor's lodgings, found some of his dearest places of refuge at manor-houses all over the country, especially on the big estates in Zealand of Gisselfeld, Bregentved and Basnæs. Many of the owners who showed him hospitality were themselves interested in art and poetry, and their homes were often small centres of culture which formed a kind of link between town and country. In literary circles in Copenhagen, Andersen was often the object of more or less well-founded criticism, and adversity of every kind he took deeply to heart. He therefore enjoyed the fuss made of him on his visits to the country, and the manor-

35. Funen. The Manor-House of Glorup

CHR. BANG

houses occupy a prominent place in his portrayals both of the Danish countryside and the Danish people, but it must not be forgotten that there are more descriptions in his fairy-tales of small rooms than of great halls, of modest dwellings than of noble mansions, and his characters are much more often poor than rich. The shoemaker's

36. Farm in Zealand

37. Zealand. The Manor-House of Gisselfeld

son from the poor part of Odense acquired surprisingly quickly a courtier's skill in treading on polished floors and mixed in distinguished company as an equal. But though he might be impressed by the grandeur and magnificence he met, he retained his natu-ral dignity. He never toadied to the great nor disowned his origin either in word or deed. There is social perspective, often social pathos in his writing. It rests on under-standing of and sympathy with the small and humble in society. With his subtle

38. Zealand. Park of the Manor-House of Bregentved

humour he has on several occasions stressed their human worth in contrast to the rich and well-born. But Andersen was no social revolutionary and he enjoyed his pleasant holidays as a guest at the manor-houses with a clear conscience. He himself wrote of them: "There I could give myself completely over to Nature, to walks alone in the woods and to social life in the manor-house, there I first really came to know the Danish countryside, and there I wrote most of my fairy-tales. — Nature around me and within me preached to me my mission."

39. Zealand. Gate at the Manor-House of Basnæs

AAGE KNUDSEN

"Near the Great Belt (the sound between Zealand and Funen) there stands an old mansion with thick red walls," so wrote Hans Andersen in the opening sentences of "The Wind Tells About Valdemar Daae and his Daughters". It tells the story of a medieval squire in the noble castle of *Borreby*. It was one of the manor-houses which Hans Andersen did not visit, but he was familiar with it and with its history from his many visits to the neighbouring manor of Basnæs, and by his story he has made the name of Borreby famous.

40. *Zealand. The Manor-House of Borreby*

Hans Andersen was a guest at thirty larger and smaller Danish manor-houses in all, and many of them became a kind of home for him where he found that peace and quiet for work which the restless life in the capital could not give him. To *Holsteinborg*, on Zealand's west coast, not far from Slagelse, which held such bitter memories from the tread-mill

AAGE KNUDSEN

41. Zealand. The Manor-House of Holsteinborg

42. Zealand. Scenery near Holsteinborg

of his school-days, he came especially in the later years of his life, and here he also spent long periods during the winter. At Holsteinborg, a manor-house with four wings, whose buildings date partly back to 1600, there still exists a room kept in memory of the famous guest. During his visits to Basnæs and Holsteinborg Hans

Andersen became closely familiar with the countryside of South Zealand and the local traditions. One of his short stories, "Vænö and Glænö", originated as an impromptu toast at a dinner party at Holsteinborg given in honour of some engineers who were engaged in connecting the nearby island of Glænö with Zealand.

43. The Island of Glænö off Holsteinborg

AAGE KNUDSEN

Mention must be made of another of the South Zealand manor-houses, *Nysö,* where Andersen was a frequent guest during the years 1838-45. Among the artists who gathered here was also the great sculptor Bertel Thorvaldsen, who had spent his manhood in Italy, but who lived in his native country during the last part of his life. At Nysö Thorvaldsen became almost a member of the family, a little studio was built for him in the park, and every

44. Zealand. From the Garden of Nysö

AAGE KNUDSEN

AAGE KNUDSEN

45. Zealand. The Manor-House of Nysö

evening lotteries were arranged for his entertainment in the garden-room. Andersen did not particularly enjoy these games, but Thorvaldsen and he were on very friendly terms with one another, and when he read his tales aloud the sculptor was always one of the most eager listeners. Some of Andersen's most famous fairy-tales such as "Ole Lukoie" and "The Bell" were written during his visits to Nysö.

46. South Jutland. Augustenborg Castle

On his foreign travels Andersen was received by many crowned heads. He was also on friendly terms with the Danish king, Christian the Eighth. It was he who in 1819, when he was governor of Funen, had received the fourteen year old Hans Andersen and advised him to become apprenticed to a trade. In 1844, twenty-five years after he had set out, alone and friendless, for Copenhagen, he was invited by the King and Queen to accompany them on a journey to the then Duchy of Slesvig, through which later the frontier between Denmark and Germany was drawn. On the return journey he paid a visit to the Duke of *Augustenborg* on the island of Als, and the next year he visited the Duke at another of his castles, *Graasten,* now the summer residence of the King of Denmark. Here he finished his story "The Little Match Girl". The bitter strife, political as well as national, which at that time was raging in the frontier district, was the cause, some years later, of the war between Denmark and a number of the German federal states — with the Duke of Augustenborg as one of the ringleaders on the German side.

47. South Jutland. Graasten Castle

48. *Jutland. The Manor-House of Nörre Vosborg*

BROR BERNILD

Last among the manor-houses which Hans Andersen visited or wrote about must be mentioned *Nörre Vosborg.* It lies, surrounded by ramparts and moats, in western Jutland, among scenery of quite another type than that of the Danish islands. The greatest contrasts in scenery to be found in Denmark are in Jutland. On the eastern side, where the coast is broken by a number of fiords and bays, one finds the same

49. A Scene from Jutland

bright beech-woods and luxuriant fields as in Zealand and Funen, except that there is a grander character about the East Jutland landscape with its broad ridges of hills which sweep in gentle curves down to the fiords or the many lakes. But on turning westwards the deciduous woods disappear and their place is taken by plantations of windblown conifers, or by great open flat stretches whose monotony is of-

TH. ANDRESEN

50. Jutland. From the Dunes of the Skaw

ten broken only by the grave-mounds from olden times. Most of the west coast is flat and there are hardly any natural harbours. Along the beach stretches a belt of ragged dunes where only the hardy lyme-grass and sea-bent can grow. To the north the peninsula tapers into the narrow spit of sand, *the Skaw*, where two seas meet, the Kattegat and the Skagerrak. Nowadays most of Jutland is under cultivation, but in the first half of the 19th century large parts of the peninsula formed a kind of desert with bogs and heather-covered moors. There were long distances between the inhabited places, the roads consisted of two sandy wheel-tracks, and the population, who mostly either won a livelihood by farming the moors or by fishing, led a harsh and meagre existence. Seen from the capital the interior of Jutland was a distant

51. From the West Coast of Jutland

52. The River Gudenaa near Silkeborg

and unknown world. Many educated men of rank who were stationed as public officials at these outposts of civilisation considered it to be an exile. Hans Andersen, the tireless traveller, was one of the first writers who toured this part of the country and wrote about its scenery and the life of its inhabitants. In the districts of wood and moor round the river *Gudenaa* he laid the scene of the tragic story of the children

53. *Jutland. The Manor-House of Börglumkloster*

"Ib and Little Christine", the poor fisher-folk from the west coast he has described in "A Story from the Sand Dunes", and about the old monastery and episcopal residence of *Børglum* he wrote the historical story "The Bishop of Börglum and his Men". The whole peninsula of Jutland is commemorated in one of his most popular songs which begins: "Jutland is laid like a runic stave between two seas. The runes are the grave mounds amid the magnificent woods and on the mighty heath, where the desert mirage dwells."

GEORG PE

Altogether Hans Andersen spent fifteen years of his life travelling at home and abroad. But however often and however far he travelled, Copenhagen was always his regular starting-point and the place to which he returned. In his fairytales and historical stories we find countless references to or direct descriptions of places in Copenhagen. Most well-known is, no doubt, the reference in "The Tinder Box", where the biggest of the three dogs sitting on the money-chests in the underground hall, is described as having eyes as big as the *Round Tower*. This tower, which is one of the strangest buildings in the centre of Copenhagen, dates from the 17th century and is joined to a church, but its purpose was to provide a centre for astronomical observations.

54. Copenhagen. The Round Tower

55. Copenhagen. The Spiral Ramp in the Round Tower

Up through the *Round Tower* leads not a staircase but a broad, paved, spiral ramp. Tradition has it that the Russian Czar Peter the Great, when on a visit to Copenhagen in 1716, rode to the top, while the Czarina followed in a coach. From the ramp there is access to the loft of the Church of the Trinity where the University Library was housed for a time. Hans Andersen came here to borrow books during his first years in Copenhagen. In his novel "To be or not to be", he makes the main character spend his childhood in a little flat at the top of the Round Tower.

AAGE KNUDSEN

56. Copenhagen. Street-sign in Hyskenstræde

An amusing and home-like feature of the street-scene in Copenhagen in Hans Andersen's time was the many skilfully made signs, by which craftsmen and tradesmen recommended their wares to the attention of the passers-by. "And at the same time you could learn what sort of people lived inside the houses, for they had hung their own signs outside. That is a very good thing; in a large town it is instructive to know who lives in all the houses." These innocent remarks are found at the beginning of the humorous story "The Storm Shifts the Signboards", which tells how a terrible gale moved all the signs around one night and showed much taunting impudence. The next day the poor town-dwellers were quite bewildered. There were people who mistook the church for the theatre, the billiard club for the grammar school; "and that was really awful."

In the old parts of Copenhagen the houses are built close together, and if one climbs a little, one has a view over a whole labyrinth of red roof-tops. But it is not everyone who is pleased to see things from above. In the fairy-tale "The Shepherdess and the Chimney-Sweep" Hans Andersen tells the story of the two small china figures from the parlour who one evening set out on their journey into the wide world. They reach the top of the chimney where all the roofs of the town lie spread beneath them, but it proves too much for the little shepherdess; she feels faint, and to her sweetheart, the chimney-sweep, she says the immortal words: "I have followed you faithfully out into the wide world, and if you love me the least bit you'll take me right home."

AAGE KNUDSEN

AAGE KNUDSEN

58. Copenhagen. The Old Frederick's Hospital

The old *Frederick's Hospital* is separated from the street by a high railing and this railing plays a part in an amusing episode in the skittish and imaginative fairy-tale "The Galoshes of Fortune". In this story Hans Andersen satirizes, among other things, the romantic admiration for the Middle Ages, which was the fashion at the beginning of the 19th century. Although many of his stories have historical themes, he did not lack an eye for the poetry in the times in which he himself lived. He took a lively interest in all the modern technical discoveries. His enthusiastic description of his first journey by that mechanical wonder — the railway — has become famous in Danish literature.

One of the most popular places for an outing for the inhabitants of Copenhagen in Hans Andersen's younger days was the park of Frederiksberg Castle, where King Frederick the Sixth lived with his court during the summer months. On Sundays one could see the popular monarch, in admiral's uniform, being rowed round the park's narrow canals in a splendid boat, while his faithful subjects lined the banks, bowing and curtseying respectfully. *Frederiksberg Park,* which is now surrounded on all sides by the town, is still the finest laid-out park in Copenhagen, with its long vistas and wide lawns. Hans Andersen mentions it in many of his stories, for example in the charming fairy-tale of flowers and children, "Little Ida's Flowers".

59. Copenhagen. From Frederiksberg Park

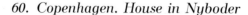
60. Copenhagen. House in Nyboder

The old quarter of *Nyboder* (New Dwellings) lies like a little idyllic provincial town in the middle of the capital. It gives the effect of being at one and the same time historical and modern with its parallel streets of undetached yellow one-family houses, all alike, of which the first were built in the middle of the 17th century as dwellings for naval men. Behind the houses are very small gardens, and in the fairy-tale "The Elder-Tree Mother" Hans Andersen tells of an old seaman and his wife who are sitting under an elder tree in Nyboder looking back over their lives. The tree spreads its branches over them, and in the tree a good fairy is hiding, whom some people call the Elder-Tree Mother and some the Dryad, while her real name is Memory. It is she who helps to make our lives full and complete.

61. Zealand. Old House in Köge

The countryside surrounding Copenhagen also provided Hans Andersen with themes or settings for many of his stories. In *Köge*, a little coastal market-town south of Copenhagen, he has laid the scene of his story "Under the Willow Tree", one of the tales of unrequited love which occur so often in Hans Andersen's writings.

ERIK HANSEN

62. *Copenhagen. Vartov*

"Near the green ramparts that run around Copenhagen is a large red house with many windows. These are garnished with balsams and boy's love; but the rooms within are bare and rude, for poor folk live there. This place is called Vartov." The green rampart has now disappeared, but *Vartov,* for several centuries an institution for sick and aged people, still exists as a characteristic part of the Copenhagen scene. It was here that Hans Andersen found his subject for his idyllic and tragic portrayal, "A View from Vartov's Window."

63. Copenhagen. Thorvaldsen's Tomb

"A big house of many colours stood by the palace and the canal, where there were vessels laden with apples and pottery. Its windows were wider at the bottom than at the top. In the courtyard there were palms and green foliage painted on the walls, and in the middle of the courtyard stood a big blooming rose-tree that spread its fresh green branches, with their many flowers, over a grave." This is a description from one of Hans Andersen's stories, "The Neighbouring Families", of *Thorvaldsen's Museum,* in the courtyard of which the famous sculptor lies buried. Hardly any Danish contemporary is mentioned so often in Andersen's writings as Thorvaldsen, who appears as the chief character in "The Porter's Son" and "Children's Prattle". He was one of the most illustrious figures of that time, and Hans Andersen felt a close attachment to him because they both had been born into poor homes and had similar fates.

64. Copenhagen. Sökvæsthuset in Christianshavn

There were other famous people of the time with whom Hans Andersen stood on a less friendly footing. Among these was Denmark's other world-famous literary figure, the philosopher Sören Kierkegaard. He made his debut as a writer with a little book which made a sharp attack on one of Andersen's novels. The leading critic and arbiter of taste of the day, J. L. Heiberg, who was manager of the Royal Theatre for many years, on several occasions assumed a rather cold attitude towards Andersen, who as a writer for the theatre, however, did not reach any great heights. But relations between them were not more strained than that Andersen was a frequent guest in the garden wing of the old rococo house, *Sökvæsthuset*, the home of Heiberg and his wife, the celebrated actress Johanne Luise Heiberg, where the elite of Copenhagen's cultural life used to gather.

65. *Copenhagen. Nyhavn*

Hans Andersen's life was characterised by his restlessness and his constant desire for change. He never had a real home; in Copenhagen he lived at hotels or rented a few modest rooms, now in one part of the town now in another. It suited his bird-of-passage nature best not to be bound too strongly to earthly possessions. "I am weighted down to earth by furniture, beds and rocking-chairs, to say nothing of books and pictures," he sighed once when he was moving to new lodgings. He lived in a great many places in the capital; in one street

Nyhavn (New Harbour) in no less than three different houses. Nyhavn is one of Copenhagen's liveliest quarters where the harbour stretches an arm far into the town. It was while he was living at No. 20, Nyhavn, that he wrote his first fairy-tales. Nearly a generation later he moved into the next-door house No. 18. These were his last lodgings in Copenhagen.

66. *Hans Andersen's Window,*
No. 20, Nyhavn

After being in delicate health during his last years Hans Andersen died on the fourth of August 1875 at a country house just outside the capital, the home of one of the Copenhagen families, which towards the end of his life had taken the place of a family of his own. A week later he was buried from the *Cathedral of Our Lady*. King Christian the Ninth and a great throng of people were present. He had no near relations to attend the funeral, but the whole country sorrowed over his death. At the funeral service one of his own poems "A Poet's Last Song" was quoted. It ends with the words: "Bear me away, O powerful Death, although Earth is pleasant. Thanks be to Thee, O God, for Thy past gifts, and thanks for those yet in store."

67. Copenhagen. The Cathedral of Our Lady

DIGTEREN

HANS CHRISTIAN

ANDERSEN

F. 2DEN APRIL 1805,

D. 4DE AUGUST 1875,

DEN SJEL, GUD I SIT BILLEDE HAR SKABT,

ER UFORKRENKELIG, KAN EI GAAE TABT,

VORT JORDLIV HER ER EN EVIGHEDENS FRØ,

VORT LEGEM DOER, MEN SJELEN KAN EI DØE.

H. C. A.

AAGE KNUDSEN

68. Copenhagen. Hans Andersen's Tomb in Assistens Churchyard.

Portraits of Hans Andersen

Illustrations to the Fairy-tales

From "Hans Andersen's House", etc.

Ab. 1835 Painting by N. P. A. Bentzen   *Frederiksborg Museum*

1845 Painting in water-colours by Karl Hartmann
H. C. Andersens Hus

1858 Lithograph from daguerreotype

1860 Photograph, Munich   *H. C. Andersens Hus*

Ab. 1865 Photograph   *H. C. Andersens Hus*   Ab. 1868 Photograph

1869 Painting by Carl Bloch   *Privately owned*   Photograph from the last years of Andersen's life

Title-page to the first
three numbers of the
fairy-tales, 1835-37.

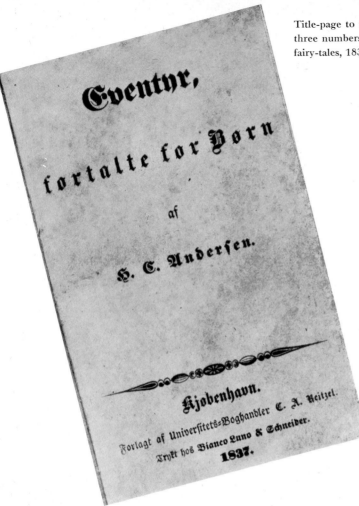

"The Little Mermaid" by the first
illustrator of the fairy-tales,
Vilhelm Pedersen, 1849.

"The Shepherdess and the Chimney-Sweep"
by Jensenius (Danish), 1949.

"The Nightingale"
by W. Heath Robinson
(English)

"The Ugly Duckling"
by Gustave Sus (French).

"The Emperor's New Clothes"
by G. Osterwald (German), 1839.

"The Tinder Box"
by Duilio Cambellotti (Italian).

H. C. ANDERSEN

BAŚNIE

TOM SZÓSTY WYDANIA ZBIOROWEGO

"Little Claus and Big Claus"
(Polish), 1931.

"The Snow Queen"
by Hauman (U. S. A.), 1942.

"The Snow-Man" (Japanese).

"The Story of a Mother"
(Bengali), ab. 1858.

"The Bell Deep" by Fritz Kredel (American),
from the translation by Jean Hersholt, 1948.

Hans Andersen's Desk in
"H. C. Andersens Hus" in Odense.

"The Little Mermaid" on Langelinie in Copenhagen.
Modelled by Edv. Eriksen, unveiled in 1913.

Statue in the King's Park
in Copenhagen.

*Modelled by Aug. Saabye in
1877, unveiled in 1880.*

The Hall of
"H. C. Andersens Hus"

*With Th. Stein's design for a
monument, 1875.*

From the Annual Transmission over the British and American
Radios from "H. C. Andersens Hus"

*Michael Redgrave reading "The Emperor's New Clothes"
sitting at Andersen's desk (1950).*

From the Theatre Museum
(the Court Theatre) in Copenhagen.

*On the wall a lino-cut portrait of
Andersen by k. j. almqvist, 1930.*

This book
has been set up in Baskerville roman type and
printed by Bondes Bogtrykkeri.
Design by Børge Christensen.
The clichés have been made by Carlsens Clichéfabrik
and the binding is by F. Müllers Bogbinderi.